WHY DO ANIMALS SLEEP THERE?

Sam George

Rourke
Educational Media

rourkeeducationalmedia.com

Teaching Focus:

Consonant Blends: Look in the book to find words that begin with a consonant blend such as *sl, cl,* or *sh.*

Before Reading:

Building Academic Vocabulary and Background Knowledge

Before reading a book, it is important to set the stage for your child or student by using pre-reading strategies. This will help them develop their vocabulary, increase their reading comprehension, and make connections across the curriculum.

1. Read the title and look at the cover. *Let's make predictions about what this book will be about.*
2. Take a picture walk by talking about the pictures/photographs in the book. Implant the vocabulary as you take the picture walk. Be sure to talk about the text features such as headings, Table of Contents, glossary, bolded words, captions, charts/diagrams, and Index.
3. Have students read the first page of text with you then have students read the remaining text.
4. Strategy Talk – use to assist students while reading.
   - Get your mouth ready
   - Look at the picture
   - Think…does it make sense
   - Think…does it look right
   - Think…does it sound right
   - Chunk it – by looking for a part you know
5. Read it again.
6. After reading the book complete the activities below.

Content Area Vocabulary
Use glossary words in a sentence.

alert
burrow
drift
habits
noble
scavenge

After Reading:

Comprehension and Extension Activity

After reading the book, work on the following questions with your child or students in order to check their level of reading comprehension and content mastery.

1. *Name two animals that sleep with one eye open.* (Summarize)
2. *Why do sea otters hold hands when they sleep?* (Asking questions)
3. *How many minutes a day do giraffes sleep?* (Text to self connection)
4. *Why do you think brown bats sleep up to nineteen hours a day?* (Inferring)

Extension Activity

Pick your favorite animal from the book. Using the Internet to gather more information about it, print pictures of the animal and glue them onto a piece of poster board. Under each picture write an interesting fact you've learned that wasn't in the book. Share this Animal Fact Sheet with your friends and classmates!

Table of Contents

Staying Alert

Animals need sleep, just like you and me. Some sleep a lot, some only a little.

We sleep in beds, keeping cozy and warm.

Maybe our pets, our cats and dogs, sleep on beds as we do.

Ducks, when they sleep, work together like a team. Line up! One, two, three.

Ducks line up to sleep. The duck at the end of the line keeps one eye open to look for predators.

A line of ducks is called a clique.

When dolphins sleep, it is called logging. Like ducks, they close one eye and keep the other eye open. They stay **alert** for other dolphins and sharks.

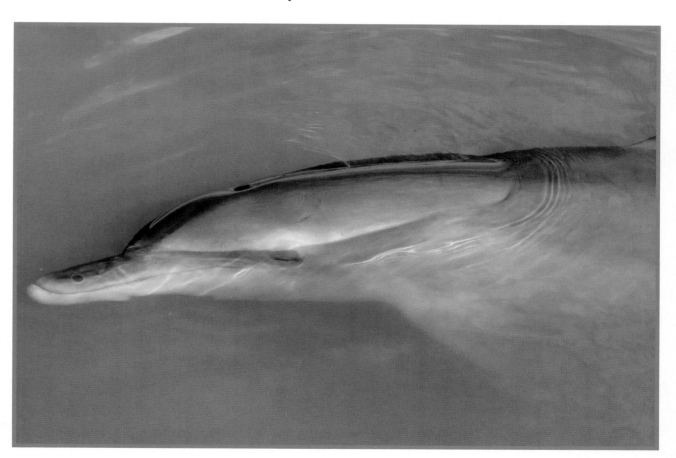

Working as a Team

Animals' sleeping **habits** help keep them safe.

Sea otters lay on their backs while they sleep. They hold hands so they don't **drift** apart.

Meerkats team up, too. Deep in their **burrow** they sleep in a pile. Their leader sleeps at the bottom, where it is warm and safe.

Giraffes hardly sleep at all. They need to stay alert for predators. For 20 minutes, they curl up on the ground and curve in their long, beautiful necks.

Can you think of a predator the giraffe might need to watch for?

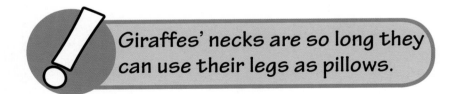

Giraffes' necks are so long they can use their legs as pillows.

Sharks sleep even less than giraffes. This is not because they are afraid of predators. It's because they need to keep moving to breathe.

Sharks swim while they sleep.

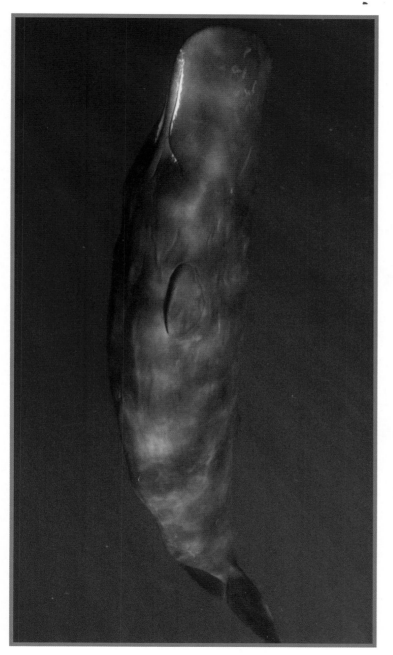

Sperm whales sleep for about 12 minutes at a time. They sleep straight up and down, bobbing along in the water.

Brown bats spend more time asleep than awake. They sleep upside down for about 19 hours every day.

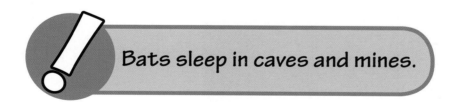

Bats sleep in caves and mines.

Nocturnal Animals

Raccoons and owls are nocturnal.
This means they sleep during the day.
They use the darkness of night to hide
while they **scavenge** and hunt for food.

Mice are also nocturnal.

Be careful, little mice.

Watch out for owls!

Flamingos are a fun bird. They do not have cozy places to lie down. They stand on one leg while they sleep!

Can you stand on one leg?
Have you ever tried to sleep while
standing on one leg? For flamingos,
it is as easy as breathing.

And what about the **noble** lion, predator of so many?

Lions do not worry about much. They sleep when they like, where they like. It is good to be a lion.

Female lions sleep less than male lions because they spend more time hunting and watching over cubs.

Photo Glossary

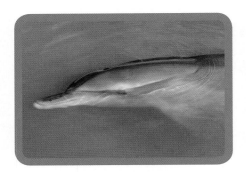

alert (uh-LURT): If you are alert, you pay attention to what is happening and are ready for action.

burrow (BUR-oh): A tunnel or hole in the ground made or used by an animal.

drift (DRIFT): When something drifts, it moves wherever the water or wind takes it.

habits (HAB-its): Things that you do regularly, often without thinking about them.

noble (NOH-buhl): Impressive or magnificent in appearance.

scavenge (SKAV-uhnj): To search among garbage for food or something useful.

Index

Websites to Visit

kids.nationalgeographic.com

www.sciencekids.co.nz

www.animalfactguide.com

Meet The Author!
www.meetREMauthors.com

About the Author

Sam George is the author of many books for kids. He lives with his family in California and spends a lot of time watching hummingbirds *zing* around his yard.

Library of Congress PCN Data

Why Do Animals Sleep There? / Sam George
(Why Do Animals...)
ISBN 978-1-68191-724-5 (hard cover)
ISBN 978-1-68191-825-9 (soft cover)
ISBN 978-1-68191-919-5 (e-Book)
Library of Congress Control Number: 2016932648

Rourke Educational Media
Printed in the United States of America, North Mankato, Minnesota

www.rourkeeducationalmedia.com

PHOTO CREDITS: Cover © superjoseph; page 4 © Pikul Noorod, page 5 © Arthiti Kholoet; page 6 © PeterVrabel, page 7 © urosr; page 8 © fred goldstein, page 9 © Jacek Jasinski; page 10-11 © davidstockphoto; page 12 © Yann hubert, page 13 © Shane Gross; page 14-15 © Krynak Tim, U.S. Fish and Wildlife Service; page 16-17 © Medvedev Vladimir, page 16 © Becky Sheridan; page 17 © Asmus Koefoed; page 18-19 © Jakez; page 20-21 © Gerrit_de_Vries, page 22 middle © Holly Kuchera; author pic © Toonstyle.com page 24
All photos from Shutterstock.com except page 15

Edited by: Keli Sipperley

Cover design, interior design and art direction: Nicola Stratford
www.nicolastratford.com

Also Available as:

ROURKE'S
e-Books